ACCENT ON
TIMELESS SONGS

ARRANGED BY WILLIAM GILLOCK

ISBN 978-1-5400-3000-9

Exclusively Distributed By

7777 W. Bluemound Rd. P.O. Box 13819
Milwaukee, Wisconsin 53213

Visit Hal Leonard Online at
www.halleonard.com

Contact Us:
Hal Leonard
7777 West Bluemound Road
Milwaukee, WI 53213
Email: info@halleonard.com

In Europe contact:
Hal Leonard Europe Limited
Distribution Centre, Newmarket Road
Bury St Edmunds, Suffolk, IP33 3YB
Email: info@halleonardeurope.com

In Australia contact:
Hal Leonard Australia Pty. Ltd.
4 Lentara Court
Cheltenham, Victoria, 3192 Australia
Email: info@halleonard.com.au

ABOUT THE ARRANGER

William Gillock (1917-1993) was born in La Russell, Missouri, where he learned

to play the piano at an early age. He graduated from college with an art degree,

but his love for music would consume his whole life. It led him to long tenures

in New Orleans and Dallas, where he was in high demand as a teacher, clinician,

and composer. In the piano pedagogy world he became affectionately known as

the "Schubert of children's composers" in tribute to his extraordinary melodic

gift. Over the years, he published numerous piano solos and ensembles for

students of all ages and levels. Today, Gillock's music remains popular in the

United States and throughout the world.

Editor's Note: The songs in this collection were arranged in the late 1970s and early 1980s as
single pop sheets. Several arrangements were updated and refined for this compilation.

Ben

Words by Don Black
Music by Walter Scharf
Arranged by William Gillock

Moderately

p

With pedal

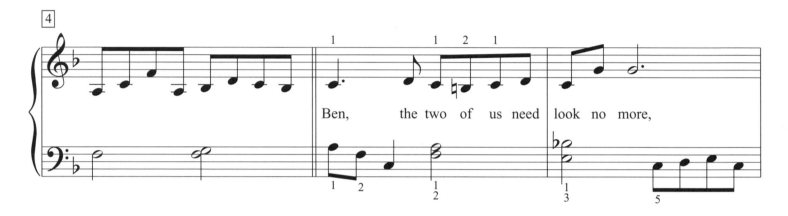

Ben,   the two of us need look no more,

we   both found what we were look-ing for.   With   a friend to call my

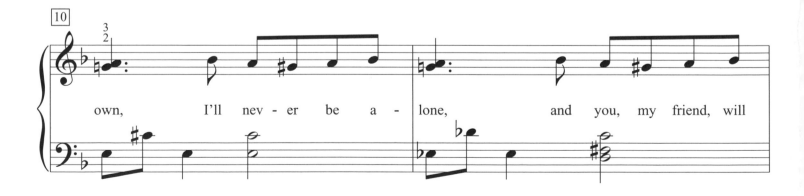

own,   I'll nev-er be a-lone,   and you, my friend, will

see, you've got a friend in me. ___

Ben, you're al-ways run-ning here and there, you feel you're not want-ed

an - y - where. If you ev-er look be-hind and don't like what you

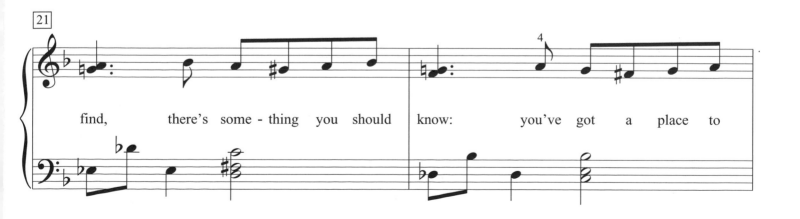

find, there's some-thing you should know: you've got a place to

go. _____ I used to say

I and me, now it's us, now it's we. I

used to say I and me, now it's us,

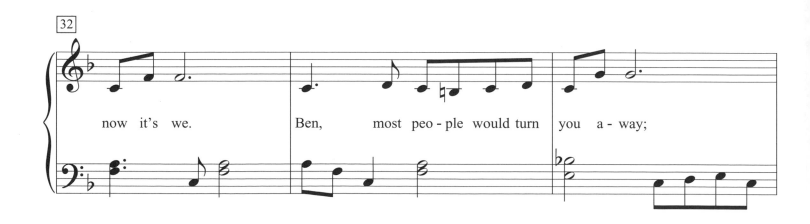

now it's we. Ben, most peo - ple would turn you a - way;

I don't lis-ten to a word they say. They don't see you as I

do; I wish they would try to; I'm sure they'd think a-

gain if they had a friend like Ben. (Like Ben) Like

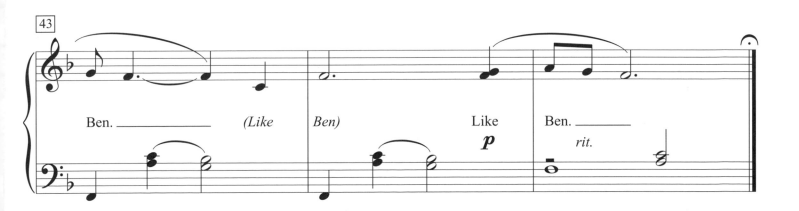

Ben. (Like Ben) Like Ben.

Cabaret
from the Musical CABARET

Words by Fred Ebb
Music by John Kander
Arranged by William Gillock

What good is sit-ting a - lone in your room?
Put down the knit-ting, the book and the broom,

Come hear the mu - sic play;
Time for a hol - i - day;

Life is a cab - a - ret, old chum,

come to the cab - a - ret.

Come Saturday Morning
(Saturday Morning)
from the Paramount Picture THE STERILE CUCKOO

Words by Dory Previn
Music by Fred Karlin

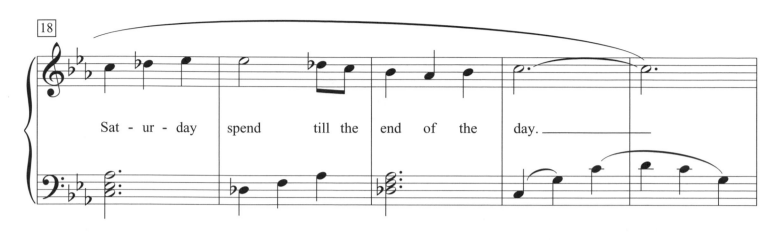

Sat - ur - day spend till the end of the day. _____

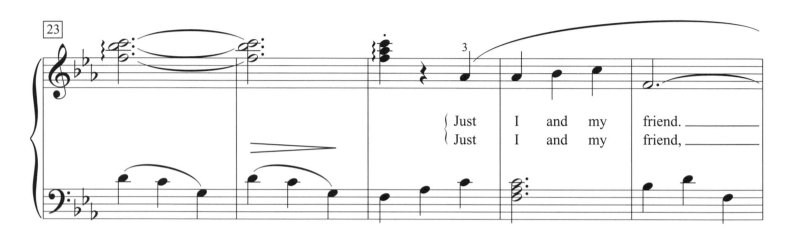

{ Just I and my friend. _____
{ Just I and my friend, _____

_____ We'll trav - el for miles in our Sat - ur - day
_____ dressed up in our rings and our Sat - ur - day

smiles, _____ }
things, _____ }

and then we'll move on. _____

13

But we will re - mem - ber

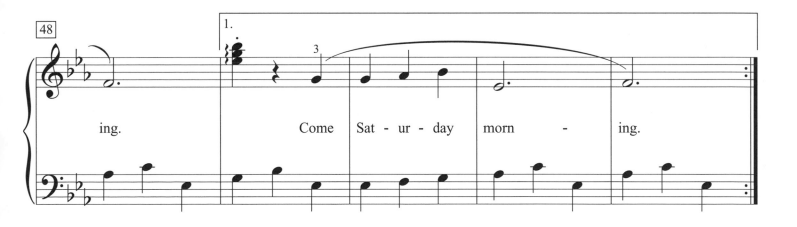

long af - ter Sat - ur-day's gone ___ come Sat - ur - day morn -

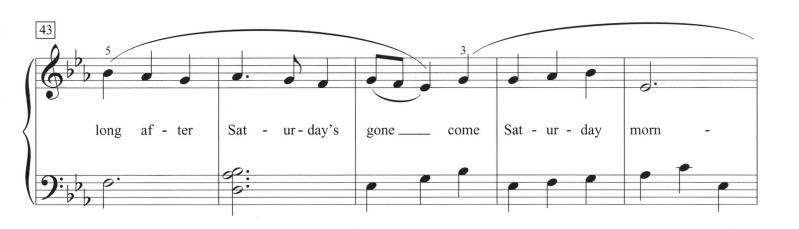

ing.　　Come Sat - ur - day morn - ing.

Repeat and fade

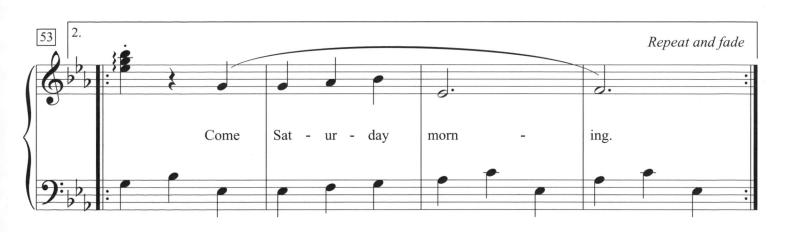

Come Sat - ur - day morn - ing.

Day by Day
from the Musical GODSPELL

Music and New Lyrics by Stephen Schwartz
Original Lyrics by Richard of Chichester (1197-1253)
Arranged by William Gillock

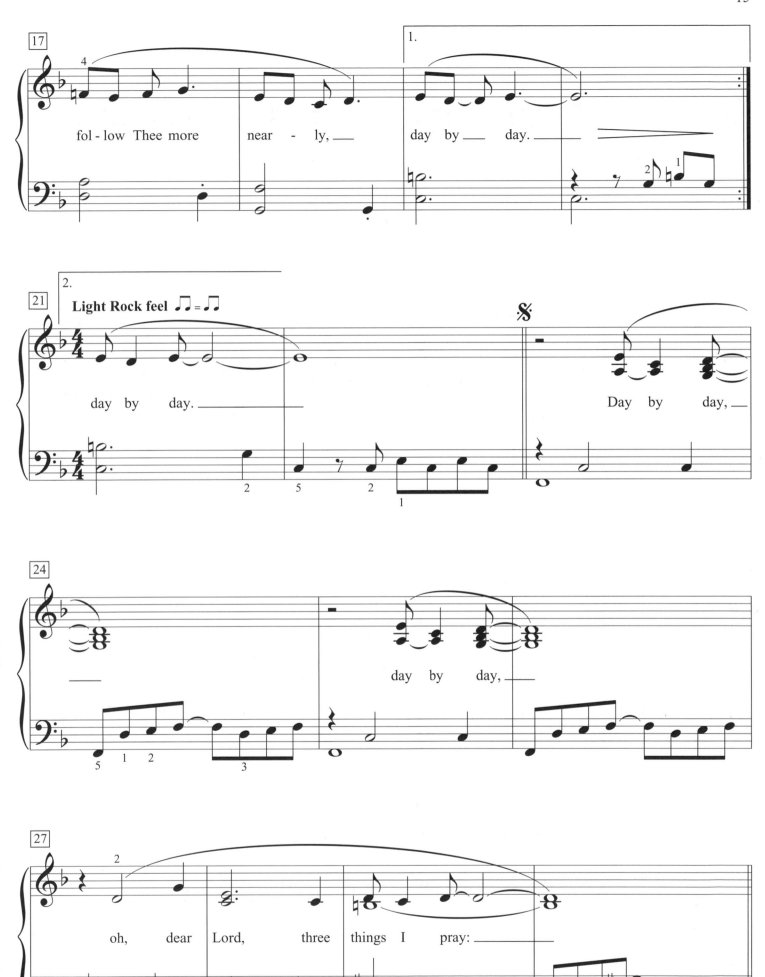

(2nd time, repeat these 4 measures 4 times)

to see Thee more clear - ly, _____ love Thee more dear - ly, _____

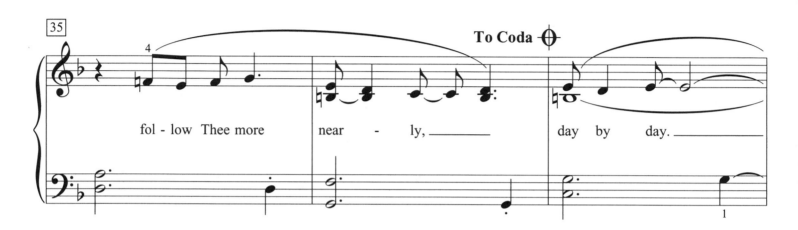

To Coda ⊕

fol - low Thee more near - ly, _____ day by day. _____

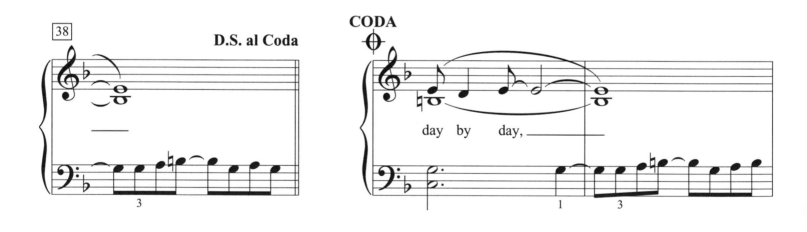

D.S. al Coda

CODA ⊕

day by day, _____

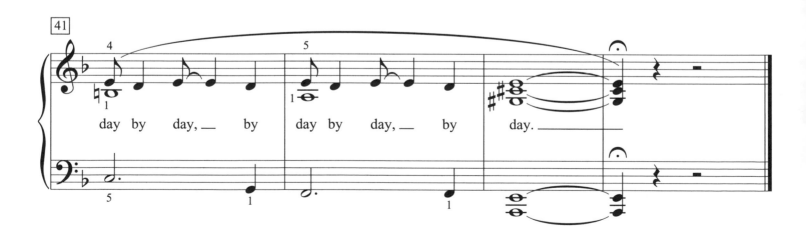

day by day, _ by day by day, _ by day. _____

Georgia on My Mind

Words by Stuart Gorrell
Music by Hoagy Carmichael
Arranged by William Gillock

With rubato

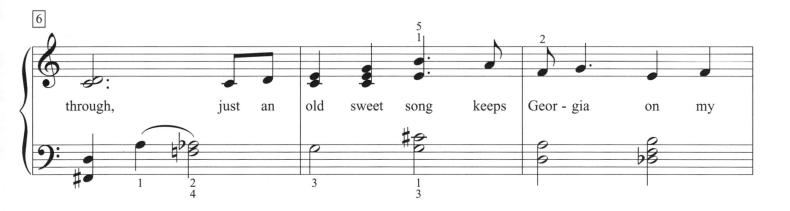

18

Each day, ___ Geor - gia, ___ a song of you comes as

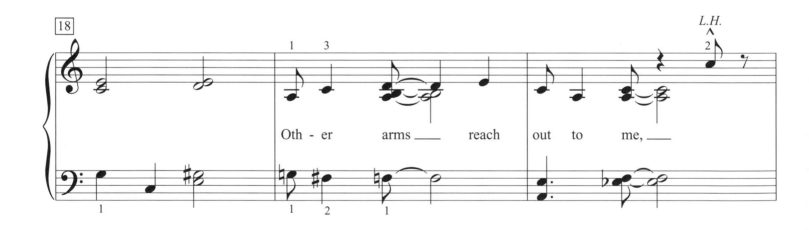

sweet and clear as moon-light through __ the pines.

Oth - er arms ___ reach out to me, ___

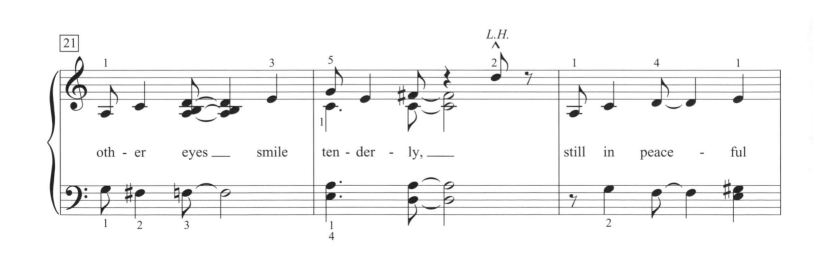

oth - er eyes ___ smile ten - der - ly, ___ still in peace - ful

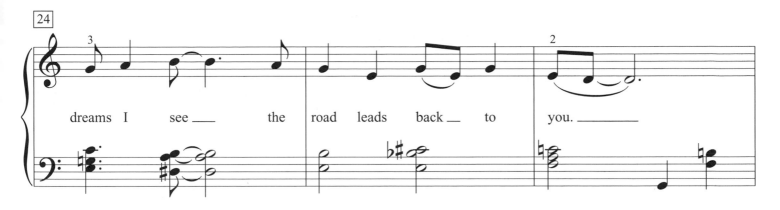

dreams I see ___ the road leads back ___ to you. ___

Geor - gia, ___   Geor - gia, ___   no peace I find,   just an

old sweet song keeps Geor - gia on ___ my mind.

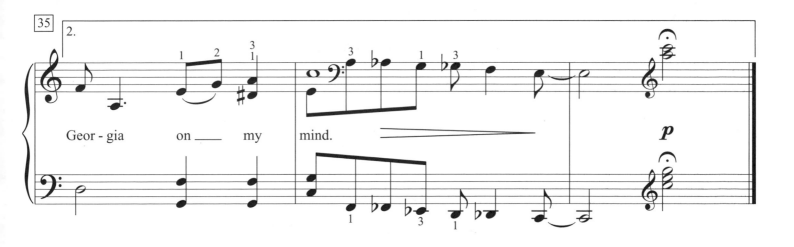

Geor - gia on ___ my mind.

p

Happiness

from YOU'RE A GOOD MAN, CHARLIE BROWN

Words and Music by Clark Gesner
Arranged by William Gillock

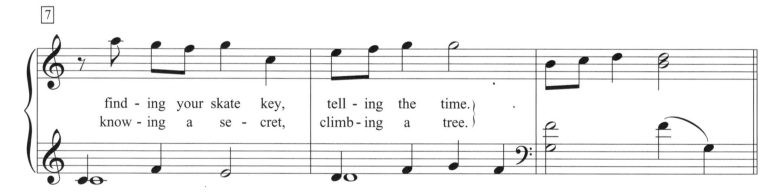

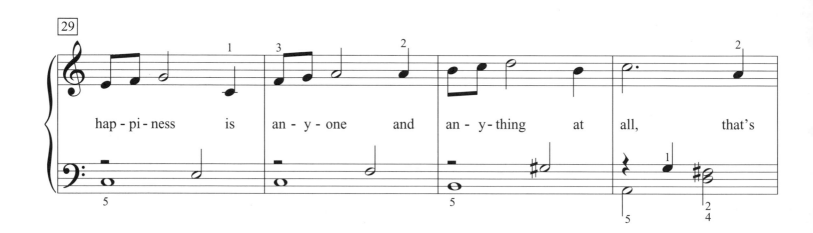

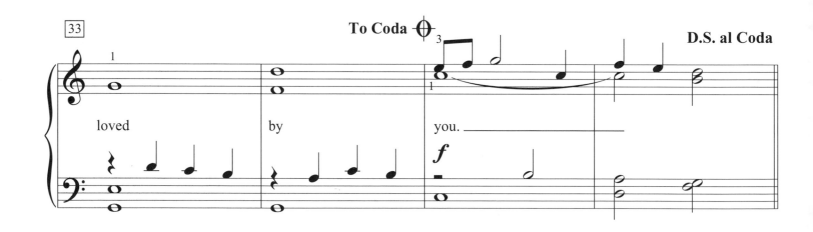

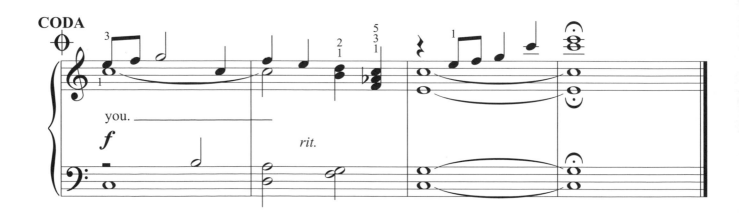

Sunrise, Sunset

from the Musical FIDDLER ON THE ROOF

Words by Sheldon Harnick
Music by Jerry Bock
Arranged by William Gillock

Moderately slow waltz tempo; soulful and wistful

Misty

Words by Johnny Burke
Music by Erroll Garner
Arranged by William Gillock

28

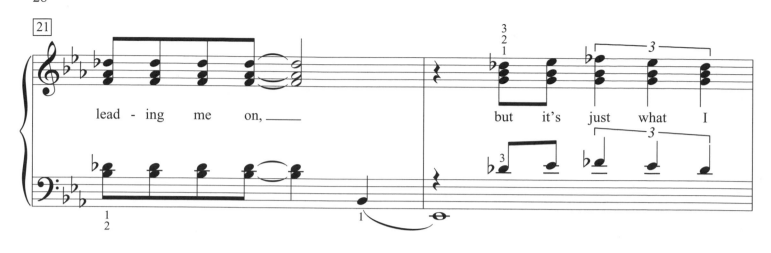

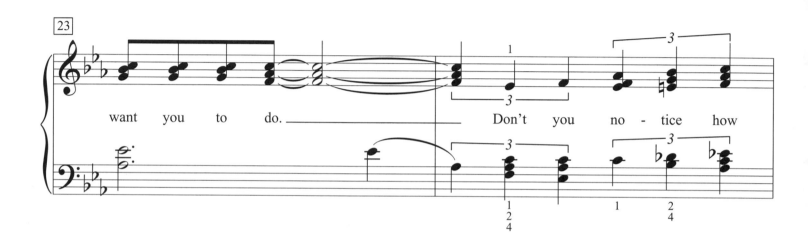

wan - der through this won - der - land a - lone, _____ nev - er know-ing my

right foot from my left, my hat _____ from my glove, _____ I'm too

mist - y and too much in love.

Look at love.

Song from M*A*S*H

from M*A*S*H

Words and Music by Mike Altman
and Johnny Mandel
Arranged by William Gillock

Moderately, Folk-Gospel feeling

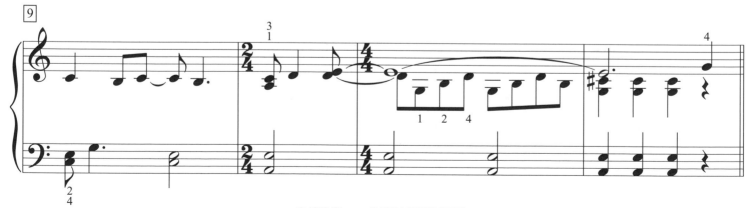

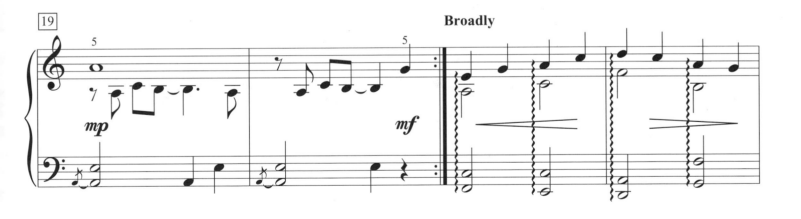

A Time for Us
(Love Theme)
from the Paramount Picture ROMEO AND JULIET

Words by Larry Kusik and Eddie Snyder
Music by Nino Rota
Arranged by William Gillock

Slowly and very expressively

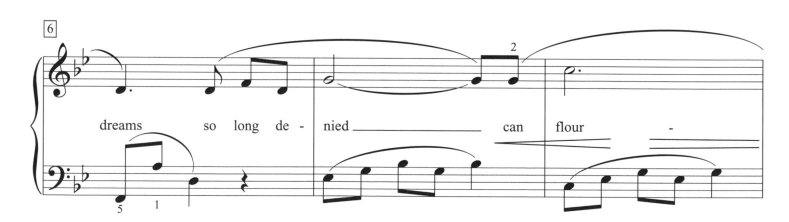

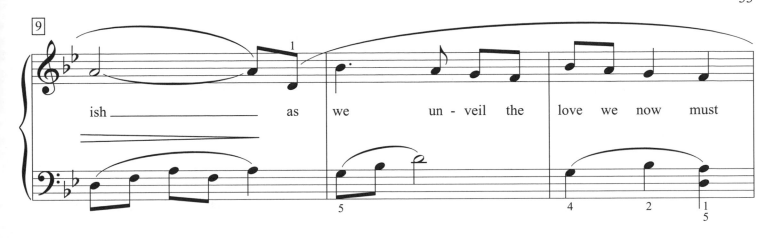

ish _____ as we un - veil the love we now must

hide. _____ A time _____ for us _____ at

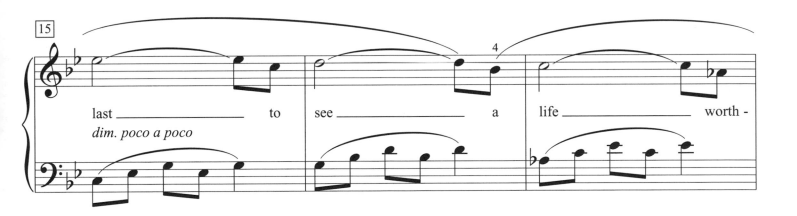

last _____ to see _____ a life _____ worth -

while _____ for you _____ and me. And with our

love   through tears and   thorns,   we will en - dure   as   we pass

sure - ly through ev - 'ry   storm.   A time for   us,   some - day there'll

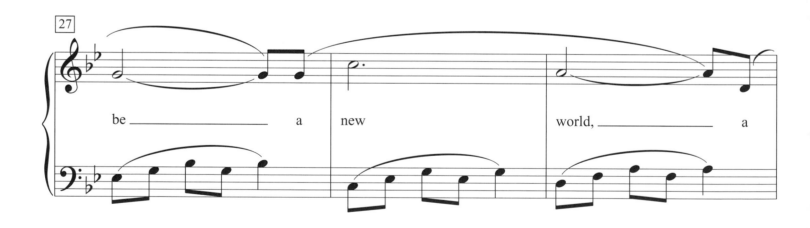

be _____ a new   world, _____ a

world   of shin - ing   hope for you   and   me.

rall.

L.H.

Where Do I Begin
(Love Theme)
from the Paramount Picture LOVE STORY

Words by Carl Sigman
Music by Francis Lai
Arranged by William Gillock

Where do I be - gin _____ to tell the sto - ry of how
With her first hel - lo _____ she gave a mean - ing to this

great a love can be, _____ the sweet love sto - ry that is
emp - ty world of mine; _____ there'll nev - er be an - oth - er

old - er than the sea, the sim - ple truth a - bout the love she brings to me? _____
love, an - oth - er time; she came in - to my life and made the liv - ing fine.

1.
_____ Where do I start?

2.
_____ She fills my

heart,_____ she fills my heart _____ with ver - y

spe - cial things, __ with an - gel songs, _____ with wild i - mag - in - ings. ___ She fills my

soul _____ with so much love that an - y - where I go _____ I'm nev - er

lone - ly. ___ With her a - long, _____ who could be lone - ly! ___ I reach for her

hand, _____ it's al - ways there. _____

mp

How long does it last? _____ Can love be meas-ured by the hou - rs in a day? ____

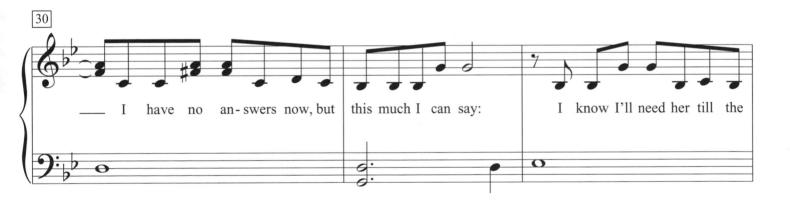

____ I have no an - swers now, but this much I can say: I know I'll need her till the

stars all burn a - way, _____ and she'll be there.

rall.

p

8vb

You Are So Beautiful

Words and Music by Billy Preston
and Bruce Fisher
Arranged by William Gillock

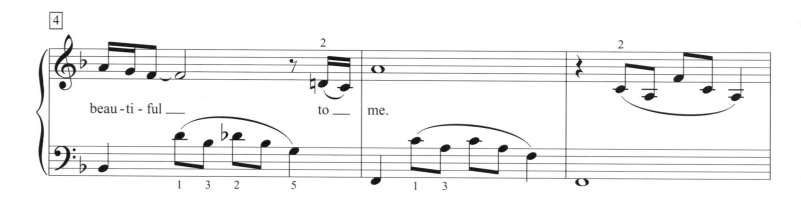

hope for, and what's more, you're ev - 'ry - thing I

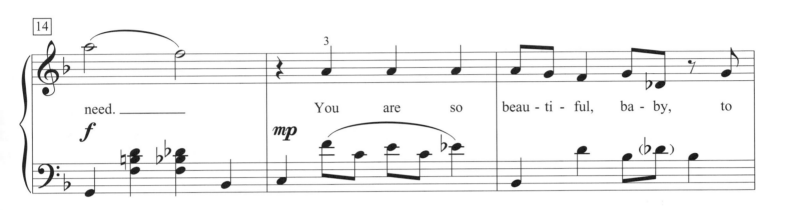

need. _____ You are so beau - ti - ful, ba - by, to

me. Such joy and

hap - pi - ness ___ you ___ bring. (I wan - na thank you, babe.) ___

Such joy and hap-pi-ness ___ you ___

bring, just like a dream. _____ You're like a guid-ing light

cresc.

shin-in' in the night, you're heav-en still to me. (Hey, babe.) ___

freely *slowly*

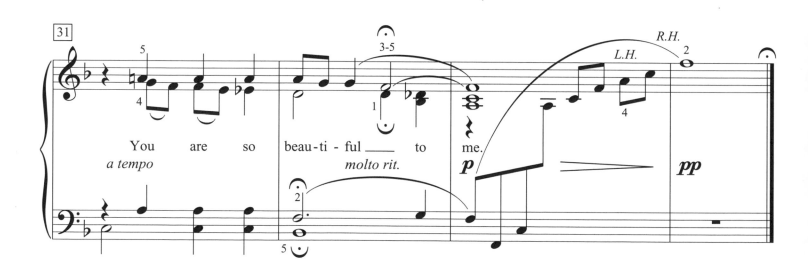

You are so beau-ti-ful ___ to me.

a tempo *molto rit.*

You're a Good Man, Charlie Brown

from YOU'RE A GOOD MAN, CHARLIE BROWN

Words and Music by Clark Gesner
Arranged by William Gillock

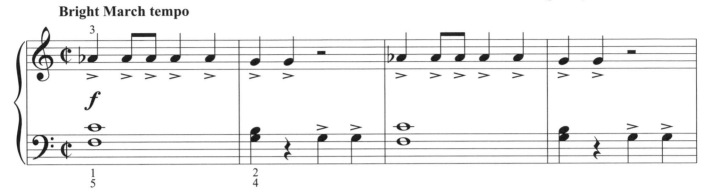

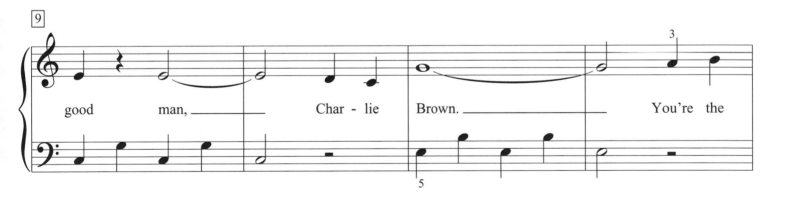

You Light Up My Life

Words and Music by Joseph Brooks
Arranged by William Gillock

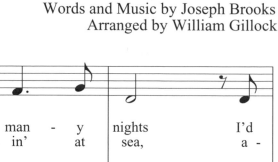

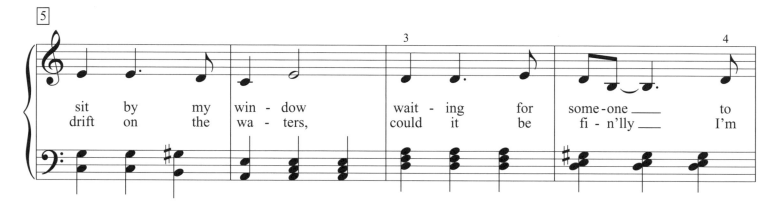

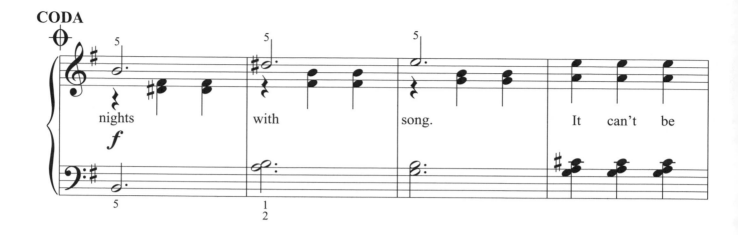

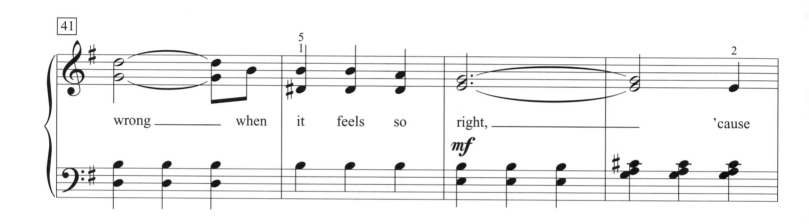

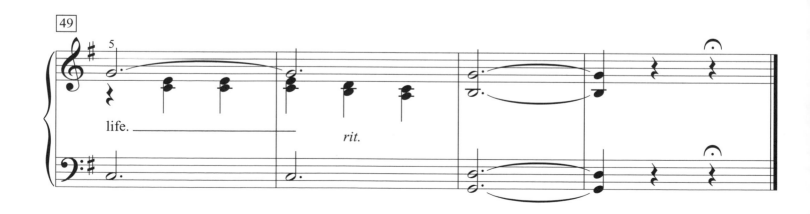